AF394193

For my family, for always supporting me.

For my new family, Robbie, for always believing in me.

And for my chosen family, Tut'Zanni, for always inspiring me.

Exploring Modern Commedia dell'Arte

A Step-By-Step Guide to Mask Work and Physical Theatre Development in Commedia dell'Arte

Table of Contents

INTRODUCTION

I've been writing down my thoughts about commedia dell'arte for a long time. I first started studying commedia almost 10 years ago, and it's changed my life and the way I think about theatre.

One thing that has always stood out to me is how fluid and adaptable commedia dell'arte is by nature. It is the reason why, as far as I believe, it was able to travel across countries and time for quite a while. Unfortunately, at some point around the 18th century, commedia dell'arte died. This was for a lot of reasons, but this book isn't really about the history, so I won't be referencing that very much.

As commedia is now slowly being unearthed, there is a lot of focus on what it was, or probably was, where it came from, etc., which is all fantastic and interesting, but having been performing commedia and developing shows on my own as well as with my company, Tut'Zanni Theatre Company, what interests me most is what commedia dell'arte would look like today if it hadn't died. Or what if it only started today? My focus isn't so much on what has already been created through it, but what more, new commedia is there still to be discovered?

Commedia dell'arte was a form of street theatre, performed for everyday people, ripe with pop culture and social commentary. So, to be true to the form, commedia should be about who we are today, and what is going on in our world. The beautiful thing is that archetypes are pretty timeless, and basic human struggles, maybe unfortunately, also seem to be the same. And that is what makes up the roots of commedia. So, we can learn about this amazing form and the crazy characters born from it, and run with the structure hundreds of years old. But we need to run from the roots, not the branches. It's not about using the same characters in the same ways with the same stories, throwing in maybe a few new jokes. That is all surface. We take the form – masked physical theatre that pulls in an audience from a core level. We take the use of archetypes: find the archetypes we see every day. Some are the same as then, but I believe we have more that are true to our time. These archetypes are what inform who the characters are. Actors and troupes created new characters all the time, and so should we. Don't be held back by "tradition"; be inspired by it. Commedia is just as adaptable now as it was at its beginnings.

We can still use basic storylines – boy meets girl, parents keep them apart, love notes are sent, notes get lost, true love is found. The truth is, the reason the storylines can be practically anything is because they don't really matter. Commedia dell'arte is not about what happens in the show, but who it happens to, inflicted by whom, and how. It is about the characters and their relationships to each other. The plot is simply a device to set up situations for us to see these relationships. This isn't necessarily unique to commedia. We love romantic comedies because we love the tension between the two characters. We love movies where the hero or heroine gains strength and stands up to their oppressive boss, or where lower class members of society pull a heist, robbing the wealthy, because we relate to these characters in some way. Commedia simply focuses on that, and uses those key points where characters come together to bring to light how we all truly feel about these issues. What's more, it is taken to the audience directly. There is no "fourth wall", or separation between the performers and audience, in commedia dell'arte. When something happens to a character, they look at the audience and make sure they saw it. They ask the audience if they saw it. Hell, they may ask the audience if they saw it and what they should do about it, and bless you (someone sneezed).

Commedia dell'arte is for everyday people, and it makes sure they are a part of it. So it just makes sense for it to be about the everyday people and the everyday world we all live in. Otherwise, why else are we doing it in the first place?

CHAPTER ONE

Getting Into Your Body

In commedia dell'arte, or any physical theatre form, it is crucial for an artist to be connected and fully engaged with their body. It seems obvious, which I suppose it is, but there is a lot involved with that, a lot more than just a mindset or a quick warm-up. Not only do we need to train ourselves to be fully engaged and present in our bodies, but we first must do a lot of un-training. Life in our modern world is not very body-friendly. We sit at computers, slouch on couches, stare down at our phones, and even though we seem to develop a lot of hand-eye coordination (yeah, video games!), there are a lot more body parts about us that require some delicate coordination as well. We store a lot of emotion and stress throughout our bodies, and don't take the time to work it out. So we slowly become tense, awkward, and very disconnected for our own bodies.

Firstly, find a body practice that suits you, such as yoga, EBAS, Alexander technique, Tai Chi, etc. Find something that isn't solely focused on the physical, mechanical form of stretching and strengthening, but also incorporates a mental aspect. Or, if you prefer, choose one that suits you, but make sure to spend time meditating while you are doing it. Pay attention to your breath. Feel hands and feet press into the floor and ground yourself. You don't have to be a very spiritual person to appreciate and benefit the full-body awareness that will result. As we develop from children to adults, there are millions of bits of fine-tuning going into muscle memory, and how our body acts and reacts to our thoughts, feeling and intentions. By taking the time to connect our minds and our bodies, it allows us to have fuller, clearer movements, and puts us back in control. We have to un-train the hunching, fidgeting, and disengagement that tiredness, weakness, and stress have programmed into our bodies.

This will not only make you a better performer, but it will protect your body and allow you to move more safely and efficiently. If a part of your body is tired, it will release that muscle group and sink into the easiest area to rest on, usually your joints, because tendons and ligaments take far less effort to hold our weight than muscles. But when we allow this to happen, it eventually wears those down, and sets us up for serious injury. Muscles can be strengthened, stretched, and even repaired much more quickly and easily than our backs, knees, and other points in our bodies where we tend to "rest".

Here are some exercises that will help you get into your body, and will support further exercises specifically for mask work and commedia. Some of these will be referenced later on, so make sure to familiarize yourself with them.

The Ant Exercise

Stand in a neutral position, feet about hips' width apart, facing a wall around 15 feet away from you. Find the point where the ceiling meets the wall, and imagine there is a small ant crawling down the wall from there. Follow it with your gaze and head. Once it passes your level gaze, hinge at the hips, and have your upper body also follow your gaze and the ant as it continues down to the floor. Continue following it as it crawls across the floor towards you and reaches your feet. By this point, you should be bent at the waist, upper body hanging.

Then, imagine the ant hops up and you catch it on your knees. Your upper body straightens back into a standing position, your feet remain planted, but your knees have now bent, popping them out in front of you. Then it hops up to your frontal hip points, which now pop forward, and the knees reset to neutral. Then to your belly. These two points are close together, so note the difference between the two. It then continues up to your chest, which pops forward. Finally, the ant hops up to your nose, where you catch and hold it until you blow the ant right back up to the top of the wall again, and you reset, watching the ant continue down the wall, etc.

You go through this process a couple of times, and then begin to speed up. First, moving quickly, but making each point a clear stop. Then moving into a fluid movement, rolling through all the points, resetting, and repeating.

Next choose a point to stop at. You can go through the points a couple of times, but settle at one. Then, as if there were a rope tied to that point, allow it to pull you through the space. Walk around, and feel what it is to move with this point being your guide. At any moment in this exercise, feel free to stop, reset (finish going through the points from where you are, blowing the ant back, hinging at the hips), and roll back up normally to a standing position. Then you can go through the points again to settle on a new one. Experiment with a few things. Even though you are leading with only one point, there are many variations you can play with. Make sure you are aware of your whole body, all the way to your fingertips. Nothing should be hanging or swinging, but should be an intentional movement.

What are your arms and hands doing? When

you walk, do you hold your arms in front of your body, or behind? Do your arms swing back and forth? Do they bounce? Think about your feet. Do your feet turn out or in, or do they point straight forward? Keep in mind that commedia characters are grounded. Don't tiptoe or stomp. Feel your feet solidly meet the ground, whether it is heel-toe, toe-heel, or flat-footed, the whole foot should press into the ground. Try to see if you can find a light-footed look while still being grounded. It is possible. Play with it.

Experiment which each option and see how it feels. What does it tell you about this character? How does the body inform your brain? Inevitably, as we move differently, we'll feel more mischievous, or curious, or nervous, or any number of personality traits. Take note of this. Take longer steps, shorter steps, quicker and slower movements, play with levels.

We are going to begin layering on concepts. In commedia dell'arte, the characters are very economical, both in thought and drives as well as movement. They don't just wander about stage. If they are moving, it is because they have somewhere to go, and they will go directly there. Think in straight lines. I am going from point A to point B. If something catches my attention, I stop, turn that way, and then continue. This is how you need to start moving in this exercise. Choose a direction, and then go in a straight line that way. Then, you can stop, turn, and go in the new direction. One thing at a time.

Remember that you are leading with a single point, so this also applies to when you are turning. You stop, then that point will initiate your turn, and the rest of your body will follow. These movements are clean. At no point should your feet be shuffling across the floor. When you are turning, your feet do not rotate on the floor. Each foot lifts, turns, and is placed back down in the new direction. To add another layer, begin to think about what is causing you to turn. What is catching your attention? Did you smell something delicious? Did you see a sexy person? Begin to think about these base drives that pull us through life. This will also begin to affect the urgency in which you change direction. Turning and going for food will be much different than looking for a bird you just heard.

Begin to vocalize. Not necessarily words, but use your breath, grunts, oohs and ahs, laughing, growls. Try to think of the actions and your physicality as informing your voice. A character leading with their gut will sound different than someone leading with their nose. A person more curled in on themselves due to pigeon toes and a hunched back will be different from someone puffed up in the chest. See how the voice differs. You can experiment with running speech, but don't get caught up in what you are saying. Again, you are allowing the body to inform your brain, not the other way around.

The next layer is the "countermask". Every person, in real life or on stage, has the version of them that they show the world. This is a figurative mask. This is the mask you wear on stage, but your whole body becomes this mask. Capitano is a proud braggart, which is why he is traditionally portrayed with a puffed out chest and a big, bravado voice. This is the "him" that he wants to show the world. But when we are confronted with negative emotional responses such as fear, anger, or sadness, more of our true selves, or our countermasks, show. This is the part of us we are trying to hide with the "mask". Capitano at his core is a coward. When confronted with a legitimate threat, he cowers away. Instead of his chest puffing forward, it sinks back, as if being tugged in the opposite direction. Each different point does the same thing, directing in on itself, and reversing in the opposite direction. Be careful of the knees, as they obviously do not bend backwards. Do not jam your knees back, be aware of them and take care. The knees are a good example where you find that moving them the opposite direction affects the rest of the body as well. Everything sort of turns and moves around this new direction.

Play with this. Move through the space, be pulled by what you see, hear, and smell, but react also with the countermask. Notice the difference between anger versus fear or sadness. These have different speeds and rhythms. Vocalize. Play with variations and see how they change how your body is informing you about the character.

If you are working with multiple people, begin to see each other in the space. React to each other. Come together, play with mask and countermask in small interactions, and then continue to move through the space. Let these moments grow, and explore them. These are the basics of character building, so find a character you want to play with and have fun with it!

The Chair Exercise

The trick of this exercise is that it is deceivingly simple on the surface, but is in reality riddled with a million challenges. Essentially, you will be entering a space, sitting in a chair, and then exiting. Sounds simple, right? Wrong.

Place a chair in the middle of a defined playing space. Make sure it is not too far from the audience. Make sure that you have defined "wings", where you know when you are definitely on stage, and when you have exited. This is an exercise that utilizes the audience, so try to have someone observe, or if you're on your own, set some objects out to represent audience members.

Enter the space. Make sure your body is engaged. Take in each audience member, and look them right in the eyes, one to the next. Now, you are going to communicate to them what you intend to do. This is very important, and will be discussed in depth throughout this book. We've discussed in the ant exercise that commedia characters are economical. They know what they are about to do and they do it. However, if you need to get across a room, if you just go in a straight line, you may run into obstacles. This is not economical. It is also difficult for the audience to follow along with what you are doing. So we break up larger tasks into smaller, bite-size pieces. We need to do one thing at a time. Entering a room and sitting in a chair and then getting up and leaving is not one thing, it is a lot of smaller things.

Choose a spot about three paces away from you that is in the direction you would like to go. This is the first part of our journey. It is simple, and more importantly, easily communicated to the audience. Look at this spot not only with your eyes, and not only your head, but adjust your whole body to be facing that direction. Basically you are indicating with your whole body to the audience that you intend to go move to that spot. Now, bring this back to the audience. You've indicated what you're going to do. I'm going to go there. Look up and make sure each audience member is with you, and you are bringing this action to them by looking them in the eyes. All of them. Check your spot again. Now, choose one member of the audience to "take with you". You are going to take those three paces and walk to that spot, but you will not be looking at where you are going or what you are doing. You have locked eyes with this one audience member. They are experiencing this single movement with you. Then, find your next action, probably a new spot three paces away. Check in with your audience. Re-establish what you're about to do. Choose another single member of the audience, and go.

Keep in mind that when you are performing,

you will have a mask on your face. The thing about masks is that they don't look as great turned away from you, and the back of your head is not pretty. Also, this is a physical form, and you want to keep this open. So you want to keep yourself as open as possible for *every* member of the audience. If you are moving from stage right to stage left, most likely your instinct is to face that way. Instead, when you are moving, choose the audience member that leaves you the most open – most likely in this situation the person farthest to the right of you. Remember you don't want to leave anyone behind.

Continue to move to your chair. Now you have the new challenge of sitting. First, you are going to have to adjust so you are facing forward, and not diagonally. Then you are going to have to get your butt in that chair. Think of these movements like when you were walking. You look at where you want to go/what you want to do, you check that the audience is with you, you re-establish what you're about to do, you choose one person to take with you, and you do it. So as you need to readjust, check where you want to face, or where you want your feet to be, check with the audience, re-check, take someone, and go. Look at the chair. Check that your audience is with you. Re-check that the chair is still there, prep your butt, choose someone, and sit. Now enjoy it. Enjoy the chair. Share that with the audience. Now, you stand,

and exit.

Note that every moment is shared with the audience. Every tiny decision, and every movement. It is very counter-intuitive to be performing actions while not looking at them (because you are looking at the audience), but with a mask, this is what works. Even when you are speaking, you look at your partner on stage, and then speak the words to them while looking out at the audience, sharing with them. Everything is a journey alongside them. It becomes so satisfying, and your audience becomes much more invested in your and your story.

This will seem tedious at first. If you can, have others watch you, and every time you make a mistake, they should clap. Applaud the mistakes. When they happen, you can react, and then reset, and try again. If you get frustrated, get frustrated. If you are confused or sad, feel it. And share it. Share it with the audience. You don't know what you did? Ask them. Be genuine. This exercise will have you begin to embrace the "flop", or failing on stage. It is so human, people can't help but watch and be engaged. Trust it.

A lot of students ask, because of the tedious breakdown of this, if we also do this when we perform. YES. It may take you 15 minutes to just sit in a chair, but if it is engaging, who cares? Your audience will not be bored. Also, begin to work faster. Push yourself. Pretend there is a bomb under your chair and you have 10 seconds to exit. This will make you mess up. You will make mistakes, become stressed and frustrated. Good. This will start to engrain the rules into your body, and train all the right habits. It will slowly become more second nature, and you will be able to control the rhythm and speed of these rules, which makes for a clean, economical, and engaging performance.

<u>The Circle Game</u>

This is by far one of my favorite games. My peers and I played a version of it in Italy where we were studying, and I've found it is one of the most valuable tools you can use for ensemble work, and in physical theatre. Plus, it's just freaking fun.

Begin in a circle, and you will want some space. This is a game of indications and permissions. One person will initiate the game. What they are going to do is look where they want to go, and that will be another person's spot. But since there is a person there, they must first ask permission to come and take their space. So they indicate, like in the chair exercise, where they want to go. Then they check through eye contact that the person is aware that they are coming to take their spot. That person must nod "yes" to indicate that they have seen them ask, and they accept. "No" is not an option in this game. It is not a competition. You want this game to go smoothly, and you want to maintain a sort of rhythm. With the "yes", the first person may now check again where they are going, and move to go take that spot.

So, now this new person knows that someone is about to come take their spot, so they need to get out of there and find a spot for themselves before they get a nice swat on the butt. But they can't go until they have somewhere to go. So they find someone in the circle, look where they want to go, get permission, check where they're going, and go. The game continues on in this way. As you get more comfortable, pick up speed. Try to get to the person's spot before they can leave so you can give them a bit swat on the behind.

This game practices tracking the focus, and supporting your teammates on stage. When you are the person who is looking for somewhere to go, if no one is paying attention or looking at you, you are left all alone, stuck. You need to support this person. The person before looked right at them to get permission to take their spot, so you know that next person is going to need to find a spot. Help them. Give them the focus, since they are the one holding the next action. You will be so grateful when it is your turn, and everyone is engaged and watching when you need them. Secondarily, if everyone who is giving focus to someone is looking with their whole body, anyone who is lost now has a whole circle of people indicating where the focus is. This is a crucial technique for commedia.

Let's add one more little layer. As part of adding clarity, we will add a little countermovement before you move from your spot. You've looked where you want to go, gotten permission, and you are about to go – before you leave your spot, lean back and gear up to go. This small countermovement will help propel you forward into your movement. It also goes along with the I-am-telling-you-what-I'm-going-to-do-before-I-do-it concept. It also helps maintain a rhythm, which is very important.

As you get a little more comfortable, it is time to complicate this exercise. Add a rhythmic song, possibly with clapping. Add a ball or two that you toss around with the same rules of getting someone's attention, permission, gearing up to throw it, and then underhand tossing it to them. Get some sticks, and pass them in a circle. Add more and more elements. What you will realize that you will create a group rhythm, and if everyone moves in that rhythm, it becomes easier and easier to maintain so many things at once, including watching for focus.

Use this exercise to create a group mentality, to connect you together, to build energy, practice clear indications and movements, and permissions. You will learn to listen to each other and the rhythm you have created. A commedia show is as rhythmic as a piece of music, and if you can maintain and control the rhythm, you maintain the energy, urgency, and movement of your performance.

CHAPTER TWO

Finding the Body of the Mask

I love the characters of the commedia world. There are actually hundreds documented, but usually there are a select few of the popular characters that pop to mind: Arlecchino (later the Harlequin), Pantalone, Pulcinella (later Punch), Colombina, Capitano. They are classic archetypes, somewhat timeless on a base level, and fantastic introductions into the world of what commedia used to be. Truly, nobody knows 100% what it was, but that simply provides a great opportunity for exploration. If we want to continue on with commedia, and let it be what it could be now in the same way it seemed to have existed and changed back then, then we must begin our own work, using basic form and technique, and see where it takes us.

The reason characters like Arlecchino and Pulcinella were so loved and popular were because first, they represented people and types of people that others could either relate to or recognize; and second, because they were created by actors who were set out to represent that archetype. That is also why the number of characters grew over the year. New actors loved this form, and created their own characters. That is what we will talk about here. I believe that if commedia had continued as it originally did today, this would be happening. In fact, it's possible that part of why commedia died the first time is because it stopped growing and adapting as it did in the very beginning, and instead people, actors, and companies started remanufacturing what was popular, churning out more profitable pieces of theatre just as we do today with sequels, spinoffs, and remakes. It stopped being created by artists who had something important to say and found a way to get people to listen (and to not be executed, or imprisoned for it) and started to be made prettier and more marketable – which also means catering to those with the money, as opposed to being for the people.

Although my company and I have taken a somewhat contemporary approach to commedia dell'arte, it is also rooted in the traditional form. I had an excellent English teacher who taught me that you must learn the rules before you can break them. That makes it so when you do break the rules, it is a choice, and for a reason. That gives it power. That makes it a choice, and not a mistake.

Let's talk about getting into a mask. I say, "a mask", and not, "the masks" because I think I've made clear previously that we shouldn't be limiting ourselves to what others have created already, or to what people say some of these masks should be (including what our own brains say they should be, intellectually).

First, choose a mask. Maybe you've borrowed one, or made one, or have one in class, whatever. Obviously, it should be a commedia mask of sorts – whether it is from an expert mask-maker, or an experimental commedia mask-maker, or even if you are yourself exploring mask creation, that's great. There are some traits I personally believe a mask should hold to be able to be used as a commedia mask. Particularly, it should be strong in style. A commedia mask is like a caricature, emphasizing prominent features, and have clear shape and lines. It should not be ambiguous in what it is trying to be. Commedia is not subtle, its characters are not subtle, and the mask certainly should not be subtle. They may have some animalistic qualities, but they should always without question be human. These all might like sound like vague or obvious things, but the mask world is huge, wonderful, and diverse. It should be. But not all those masks will work with commedia. You also may go through some trial-and-error when discovering useful masks for yourself. For the sake of learning-the-rules-before-breaking-them, if you are new to this world of commedia, or only just trying to stretch out of "traditional" commedia, try to get your hands on some masks that have some credibility. Even classic Arlecchino or Capitano masks, sure. But when you begin these exercises and work with these bad boys, forget everything you know about the traditional characters and who they are. Do not try to reproduce pictures you've seen, or performances, or things you've read.

Look at your mask. You've picked it for a reason. It stood out to you for a reason, or you should have some initial gut reactions to it. Don't put it on yet. Carefully hold it in your hands. A few words on mask etiquette – please be gentle. Be respectful. Do not hold a mask by its nose or its eyeholes. On a practical level, this is because that can wear out and break down the mask, but also, these masks have a life of their own. If you are not going to respect them, then this form will not serve you, and you will have a difficult time connecting with it.

A proper way to hold a mask for observation is as follows: hold your forearm and palm out horizontally, palm face-up. Place the mask onto your palm with the mask facing you. It should be right-side-up, like the mask is looking at you. Line the top of the mask up, so that you can curl your fingers around the top edge, fingertips pressing into the forehead of the mask. You should be able to get a secure grip so you can turn your wrist and move the mask without dropping it. Lift your arm so you are eye-to-eye with your mask. Give it a stare down. Begin to look at the mask as a whole piece. Look at how the light hits it. What shapes can you see? Are there sharp, angular lines, or are they softer and more rounded? What effect does this have as you observe it? Take note of this, and begin to look at the mask as a face. Is this an old character, or young? Smart, or slow? Again, take note of these impressions. And be a little judgy here of this character. They are supposed to be caricatures. Commedia characters are straightforward. If they look dumb, then they are probably dumb. If they look old, or fat, or naive, or mischievous, this is important.

Now bring the mask, continuing to hold it in the same manner, up next to you. Turn it side to side, up and down, as if it were looking around. Experiment with quicker and slower movements, sharper and softer. Have it move around in all three planes (up/down, left/right, forward/backward) and really look at how it looks when moving around. This is really the only chance you get to see what it looks like, because once it is on your face, even in a mirror, you won't get to see what it looks like with living movement.

Once you've had a good look at this mask, go to a mirror, and put it on. You'll probably need to use a few sponges (I recommend the little flat triangular makeup ones that are perforated, but any sponge will do) to get it to fit properly and comfortably. You want the mask to fit as close to your face as possible, with your eyes as visible as they can be. Depending on the mask, this may mean that the bottom of the mask and your upper lip don't line up properly, but it is far more important that your eyes be lined up with the eyeholes as best they can.

Once you have it on, look at how it looks on your face. It is possible that some of your first impressions will now change, and that's fine. One of the most sorrowful-looking masks I have come across actually turns to a look of pure joy when put on. Strange, but good to know. Try out a few expressions. Take in what this mask looks like on you. Then take it off again. I know, once that mask is on, the desire to play tends to rise, but you want to go in with the right form. The reason we put it on before jumping back to where we were before is so we can have the most fully-formed impression of this mask before we create their body.

We are going to go back to the ant exercise. Using the mask to inform your body: which point would this mask lead with? Find this again by looking at the lines this mask holds along with character traits. Choose a point, and begin to walk through the space, again with the mask up next to you. Connect your body and movements with how this mask moves through the space. You may have to try out a few or all of the points. Commedia is very much a process of trial and error.

CHAPTER THREE

The Focus

One of the essential elements to a successful commedia show is good control and use of focus. If you can master the focus, then you can have the audience in the palm of your hand. I'm not talking about being focused on stage, but *the* focus, the audience's focus, the focal point of all action, attention and energy.

Think about a good tennis match. The onlookers watch the game, intensely engaged, back and forth. Tennis is an excellent example of control of focus. They know where to look, and where to expect to look next. Partly because of the brightly colored ball flying around, but also because the players gear up with a countermovement, then indicate where they are going to throw - or hit, rather - that focus with a clean, powerful movement. In commedia dell'arte, you should expect no less clarity or physical output.

In commedia dell'arte, however, it's more than just back-and-forth. It's back, and forth, and held here, stolen there, and all with that same sense of urgency and engagement.

Think about your exercises. You are constantly indicating to the audience where you are going, what you are going to do – you are telling them where to look, and where to expect the action. When watching that tennis match, you aren't constantly watching that little ball. As soon as a player is swinging, you are looking to the opposite side to see what is going to happen. Because you know that is where the action is going to be.

This, on stage, is generous. It is clear. You've brought your audience into a heightened space, where characters, masks, voices, and urgency are blazing by with such energy, that the least you can do is tell them where to look. Don't let them miss a second. Be generous. Bring them with you; better yet, send them ahead. It's the only way they will feel they can catch up. Then, when there is a missed swing, or a fiasco, they really feel it.

As you begin to work on your feet, constantly think about where that focus is. I would think of it as a ball of energy – sort of like a tennis ball, but don't get caught up in thinking it has to be constantly bouncing and moving, or you'll exhaust yourself and your audience. You don't need to be trying to watch where it's going to go, you need to be in control of where it is and is going to go. You do, however, want to keep that level of engagement. But don't stress too much over that right now. Honestly, as long as you and your body are engaged, and you know exactly where that focus is, the audience will naturally be engaged. They won't be able to keep their eyes off that ball.

So. You have to enter a space, sit in a chair, and exit. Let's track the focus through this exercise. It begins with a blank space, of course, like the top of a show. The audience is open and ready. It's sort of like a soft focus on the stage. A mask enters. This immediately takes the focus, no matter what. When a mask appears, there is no way it will not pull the focus. So now you've entered. You are the focus. The inevitable movement of your entrance should have stopped by now, because as you know, it's one thing, one movement, at a time, and your entrance was it. Okay. Great. All eyes are on you. So what's next? You are going to choose your spot 3 paces away that you are going to go to. This is a thing. That spot now has the focus. If you are standing there looking at the audience, your mask is sucking up all of that focus. But your mask, as you also now know, is not just your face. It is your whole body, your whole being. So you want to give that spot the focus, because that is how your audience knows where to expect the action to go. They don't have the privilege of having 2 rackets to bounce back and forth between. So you have to build it for them.

So, since you had the focus, you now have to shine it, like a beacon of light, onto exactly where to look. Your gaze goes there. Your eyes, your intention, your energy, your primary leading point and every other point on your body and self should now be pointing, clearly, exactly where you are going to go. Not the general direction. Once there is a mask on stage, there is no more soft focus. Everything is sharp and clear. You should be looking and aiming at that point so hard that your audience can't help but look simply by reflex. They know. Then, check in with them. Don't worry, remember that once a mask appears, it snaps up that focus.

CHAPTER FOUR

Finding the Voice of the Mask

Just as much as each mask has its own body, it also has its own voice. But also, just as it is with your body, it is unique to the performer, and their relationship to the mask. There is no one voice for any character. Accents and stammers, sure, but not a voice.

A common mistake is to put on a cartoon voice when one puts on a mask and becomes a character. The impulse is not entirely wrong, as it definitely should not be your own voice. And be careful; just as our bodies sink into our actor habits, our voices develop habits as well. We must make sure we are engaged and aware of our voices. Not tense or stressed, but engaged vocally.

Finding the voice of the mask is a process not unlike finding the body of the mask (noticing a trend?). Each specific mask - not each character, but each individual mask - is unique. No matter the material, each mask has a specific resonance which will project the voice naturally and without much effort. A well-crafted mask will have lines and structures that aid in this, and I find that leather tends to be the best for this, though there are, of course, exceptions.

To find this resonance, put on the mask, and make sure it is sitting comfortably against your face. Depending on the mask, it can be difficult, but try to find a way to wear it as close to your face as possible (obviously full contact is best).

The nose frequently holds most of the resonance, both in the mask and is the easiest space to feel in our own faces. Place your thumb and forefinger of either hand on either side of the bridge of the nose of the mask, nearest the face (so not way out on a long nose). Hum a strong "M" sound, beginning at your lowest point of your range, and up to your highest, and back down (in a siren), and find where you feel the vibration with your fingers the strongest. Then, from that tone, release into a "Mmmaaa" a few times, then release into a phrase ("Mmmmild wind this evening").

You should feel that this vocal point causes the least strain on your voice, whilst still coming out loud and clear.

Experiment with how nasal the voice is, where you hold it in your throat. Even try a couple other vocal points so that you can feel and hear the difference when it is resonating and when it is not.

Use this technique each time you feel you've lost the voice. When you have it, it will help further inform your character, and a surprising amount of the performer's confidence is affected by being in the proper voice or not.

Resist the temptation to come up with a voice ahead of time. It is easy to fall into the trap of choosing what we think the character's voice should be. But choosing a shrill high voice for Strega (the old witch) not only strains the actor's voice, risking injury and creating discord between the actor and mask by not using the proper voice, but you are closing yourself off to the opportunity of finding a richer, fuller character that is true to the mask. The more harmonious the body, voice, and mask are, the more the actor disappears and only the character remains.

CHAPTER FIVE

The Audience

Let's talk about audiences. First, I want to talk about American audiences. Modern American audiences. They are a special breed. They love structure. They love knowing what to do. And they have been trained to come in, sit quietly, and safely in their seats. If food and drink are even allowed (which I think it should be, but that's a whole other topic), you are expected to unwrap your candies ahead of time, or else suffer the death stare from the other, more well-trained member of the audience. Everything is built around essentially making it seem that the audience doesn't exist. I am not critiquing this style, as it does serve some styles of theatre, but I am bringing it up because it is very important to know what you are up against when bringing them commedia dell'arte.

Commedia is a form that requires the complete opposite concept. In fact, commedia does not work or truly exist without them. Your audience is your playmate, your stage partner and essentially the batteries that can breathe life into your performance, or can quickly become a black hole which sucks away all life, energy, happiness, and probably your entire sense of self-confidence and self-worth as an actor.

And, truthfully, you are the responsible party for
either situation. You decided to bring this to them, and
it is your responsibility to take what they give you to
guide them, to mold what happens on stage to be
accessible to who you are bringing it to. Commedia is
a conversation, and you wouldn't speak Spanish in
China, then get mad at them for "just not getting it".
And, let's be honest, some people are jerks. If you
didn't know it before, you do now. I'm telling you now:
People are jerks. We all are. We are judgy, stubborn,
and hard to please. So you can either throw a pity
party, blame them for your breakdown after a failed
show, or you can take it, acknowledge it, and try to
use it to your advantage. Or, at the least, work with it.

      Commedia dell'arte died. It was gone. For a
long time. Only relatively recently has it been
rediscovered, and only even more recently has anyone
actually taken an interest in seeing it. Audiences are
just starting to get curious. A lot of people recognize
the name, but you can't really know it until you've
experienced it. We have the added challenge of mobile
phones and Google searches. It is a glorious thing that
we can look up every little thing we are curious about,
but there's nothing more difficult than someone who
"already knows" what you are supposed to be doing.
Even if they've experienced it in person, that was
someone else's version of commedia, which is
awesome, but realize you need to let your audience

know they're about to watch you and your performance with your rules.

So we've talked about our modern American audiences. I choose to use them, because honestly I think they are the most difficult. I haven't performed for all the audiences in the world and don't claim to have, but from what I have experienced, European audiences are more okay with being rowdy, Asian theatre has been using masks and physical styles for ages, and from what I can tell of those who have either never seen theatre before, or rarely have, they're a lot more willing to go along with whatever you have to throw at them, including the crazy that happens in a commedia dell'arte show.

Your toughest sell will always be the ones who already "know" how things should go. Audiences that are used to this style or something similar will go with it. New audiences are more malleable. But a trained audience doesn't just have to be trained on what to expect and how to enjoy the show, they must first be untrained from all their bad habits. This involves a lot of the carrot and a lot of the stick (though maybe a little more gently. DON'T HIT YOUR AUDIENCE MEMBERS WITH STICKS).

First off, seeing a mask on stage at all is a big thing. A mask is a huge character. It looks weird. It moves weird. It talks weird. You can't just burst right out of the gate at full-force commedia speed straight at your audience. You have to ease them into it. That is terrifying, and they will shut down immediately. Be gentle. Don't overwhelm them. It's like learning any new language: if you are clear enough and keep a good pace, your students will listen hard and carefully. They may be even more engaged than usual because of the effort it takes. Because the truth is, they want to get it. They bought a ticket and they showed up - in this industry, we know how massive that is. Yes, people are jerks, but they also don't want to look stupid. They will engage with you, and even follow your lead if you make them feel safe enough and at least somewhat in control. Just like learning any new language, if you speak it too quickly or in a complicated manner, they are likely to shut down and give up. And could you blame them? No. We all like a challenge, but no one wants to feel like they are failing. So, you've got options, and steps. I'm going to go back as far as I can in this process.

First, when you advertise your show, make sure it is clear that it is commedia dell'arte. That there are masks. I am not meaning to come across as condescending; for all I know, you may be an expert at marketing. But for everyone else, I've seen so many companies fail here, including my own at times. You'll find that a good part of setting up your audience for success involves stating the obvious facts from the beginning, just like I am here. Because, truthfully, if they already know, then they get to feel smart and be all like, "duh, of course I knew that," just like some of you will be right now reading this. That's great. Fantastic. People love to be in the know, it feels good. But don't leave behind those poor souls who have no idea what they are walking into.

Bring in the right audience. That includes those that already "know" what commedia is. Bring in those who have no idea what it is, but think it sounds cool and new and interesting, and thank heavens you told them this existed, because they wouldn't have had a chance otherwise. And, of course, it brings in those who pretend they know, but don't actually know, but since you told them, now they get to join that elite group who already of course knew, because you laid it all out for them and they quickly went home and Googled the shit out of it. Or on their phone standing in line. Whatever. We've all done it. Now everyone's on the same team. Your team. And this will be the theme and sentiment you will want to continue throughout the course of the night.

Use your programs to your advantage. Have a little bit about the style, give them a reference point for the commedia you are about to perform, maybe some ideas that you are touching on in the show, and set the tone for what's about to happen.

Next, definitely introduce your show, who you are, and what is about to happen. My guess is that if you are performing commedia dell'arte, there will definitely be some people who do not know who you are or what you do. Don't talk down to your audience, but tell them where you come from, what you're about to do, what you expect from them. Tell them this by telling them how excited you are. If they see that you are excited about it, then they will be excited about it. This form is new (for our time), and unpredictable by nature. That's not scary. It's exciting. It's going to be fun – as long as they make it fun. See, already holding them accountable. It's a joint adventure, and they have the power to launch that forward or hold it back. That is true, so it's not fair if you don't let them know it from the start.

Then you start your show. Here, I can't really tell you what to do, because it's your show. It depends on what it is, but I can give you some suggestions. Take the most intense, extreme aspect of your show. That can be a specific character, a recurring lazzo (I'll go over what a lazzo is soon, don't worry), a style choice you've made, either aesthetically or conceptually. Then, what is the most gentle, fun, and accessible way you can introduce that? For example, in Tut'Zanni's *Love Letter Lost*, probably the most intense aspects are two-fold: first, that there are a lot of characters, and they all want different things, and second, that sometimes we get a little crazy and call out on ourselves that we're being weird because under those characters are actors following impulses – in character. That sounds confusing, right? Well, it's even more confusing on stage if you're not expecting it. Also, the one thing that is hard for any commedia dell'arte show, as I've mentioned before, is that you have crazy people wearing crazy masks, acting crazy on stage!

So, our solution was simple, and actually surprised us: a song. At the top of our show, as actors unmasked (or with masks on top of our heads if need be), singing a little diddy in folk tune style, about our story. And what is any commedia story about? Its characters. So we introduced each character, who they were (a servant, a master, a lover), what they wanted, and a touch of where they were going. As we sang about each one, the actor playing that role would don the mask and the character, so the audience would get something like a living glossary of what to expect. How much more generous can we be? And it's not talking down to them, it's not pedantic and lecture-y; it is fun, upbeat, sets the tone, and gives information all at once.

Not only were we introducing the characters, but along the way, we'd act as though we kept forgetting the next verse. Now, actually, that was legitimately true some nights, but yes, was otherwise contrived (sorry to break my rule about not trying to be funny). First, now they know the basic story setup. Who wants what, who is whose parent, etc. We can only give so much, since a lot of it depends on them and their choices. But that's the beauty of commedia – all you need is a basic setup and stock characters and you're ready to go. Think of any episode of *The Simpsons*, or *Cheers*. You know the characters. Doesn't matter how mundane, or how insane the plot gets, since you know the characters, you have a reference point, and you'll go along with it. So now our audience has been set up. They know who is who, and they know we get a little tongue-in-cheek with the humor. Oh, and we forget things. That's real. And we call each other (and ourselves) out on it. This is true of the intro song, and true of the whole show. The tone has been set, and they are ready to see the show.

A song is not always the answer. For the show, we happened to use songs, music and sound throughout the entire show so it all fit together seamlessly. That's not true of every show, and a song will not always be what you need. In another of our shows, we just have one character on stage giving an introduction, with a small fiasco that mirrors a larger one. In our video game themed show, we have an 8-bit version of our storyline setup, and character setup. But each time, it is crucial to set the tone and introduce the characters, or what to expect regarding them. If you're doing it right, it shouldn't be that complicated. I had a peer tell me of a lazzo where it took 3 minutes just to pour a glass of water on stage – and that's how it should be. Pouring a glass of water in itself is not hilarious or even engaging, but if you have full, generous characters, and a baseline of fiasco, then you can have your audience rolling in their seats begging for mercy – in a good way, of course. So find what that is for your show, and give it to your audience. They need that reference point. They want to know who you are and how to understand you - give it to them. There is nothing more satisfying than an inside joke. Make it with them.

I was taught to not be mean to the audience. But I'm also pretty stubborn and like to do things my own way. Not that you make them your whipping boy, but hold them accountable for their actions. And, let's be honest, what is more human than blaming everyone else for your problems? Remember to share everything with them, take them on your journey, and discover the show together.

CHAPTER SIX

Actor Habits

We have spent our whole lives being ourselves. That is a fact. So, when we get on stage, we inevitably take a bit of that self along. This isn't a bad thing, in fact it can make a performance more genuine. But when we put on a mask, there are some bits that must be left behind. These are our actor habits, or perhaps more accurately named our human habits. This is your clenched fists, your hip pop, tapping fingers and shaking legs. The little things we do when we are nervous, tense, concentrating, or just being who we are. Remember that commedia characters are economical and straightforward. Become a blank slate, physically, before you put on a mask. Mentally you can only do so much, but allowing yourself to let go of all physical habits will give you the maximum number of opportunities, observations, and complete control of focus.

There are a million things we do on a daily basis without even realizing it. We fold our arms. We rub our fingers together. We tap our feet. There are a gazillion ticks and tocks that make us who we are. But that is not who we are supposed to be in a mask on stage. We are supposed to be Arlecchino, or Pantalone, or some new Zanni, but even a new character should be something of its own, not a version of us with a mask on our face.

For example, imagine you are looking at a blank piece of paper. If a dot or a doodle were to suddenly appear, you would notice it, and it would not only grab your full attention, but would hold it as well. Now imagine that piece of paper had a rotating flower, a jumping triangle, a winking face, cars, squiggles, and all sorts of hubbub going on. You wouldn't know where to look. Details would become less noticeable, and in fact, objects could probably appear or disappear completely without your even noticing. Commedia dell'arte works very much in the same way, both on a large scale, as well as small. The plots are simple. The characters are simple. On stage, one mask moves at a time, and they perform one task at a time, one movement at a time. This makes everything clear and strong. If you want your audience to see a tulip appear on your piece of paper, then it had better be clean and clear of any other doodles. They will know they've seen the tulip, and they will probably be able to tell you its size, color, and their personal thoughts about it.

Make your physical form as blank as that piece of paper, and everything from that point on will say something. As you find the body of the mask, it will be clear that if you are hunching, it is because you are old or injured; if your leg is shaking, it is because you are scared; if your fists are clenched, you're holding a bucket or about to throw a punch. Every part of your body must be engaged at all times. Don't be lazy. Don't be negligent. Be aware. Be present. From a position of neutrality, actions you may not even expect may happen, and inspiration is born. Remember, try to let your body inform your brain about who you are and what you are doing.

Use the chair exercise to begin with. Notice especially what your body does in moments of tension. Pay careful attention to still moments. Stillness is a powerful tool. Try to achieve it completely. Remember, commedia characters are economical. They don't have a million extraneous movements. They go from point A to point B and sit and do what they're there to do, and they leave. Do not add a layer that doesn't need to be there. DO be clean. DO be clear. DO be genuine, and DO be in the moment. Not as an actor, but as that character.

Begin the exercise. Already, be aware of your body. Your whole body, all the way through your fingertips. If your fists are clenched, unclench them. Are you pursing your lips? Breathe. Relax your tongue. Find the point you are leading with, find where you are going, share with your audience, and go. Now that you've arrived at your next point, check in again. Is your whole body engaged? As you are finding where you're going next, what does your body do? Do you adjust your clothes? You shouldn't, unless they are genuinely in the way, and if they are, then that adjustment should be a clear and deliberate choice, three times bigger than normal life. Remember that when you are performing in mask, or physical theatre in general, that every movement is a communication. Don't lead the audience astray with extraneous movement.

Notice the habits you have, but don't just abandon them and let them go too quickly. Once you are on stage, you are performing. You are a character, not yourself. So if you've noticed something, react to it. What's this? My jaw is clenched? Well, my teeth were stuck together with this toffee I was eating, so I'll just quickly finish it, swallow it, and move on. Let it go with an action, a choice. This strengthens many performance muscles: saying yes, taking opportunities, being aware (since you had to be aware enough to notice it in the first place) and allowing your body to inform your brain. Since these actions happen unconsciously, we immediately have to justify them afterwards, as opposed to a manufactured action where the idea came first.

It is very tempting to try to be funny, or weird, or to overact in this exercise, especially as you get a little more comfortable. Resist that urge. Most of the time what will kill you in commedia is if you try to be funny. When you try to be funny, everyone knows, and it is very disingenuous, and it will nose-dive your energy quicker than you can blink. Even if you are funny, and succeed, and get laughs, and everyone loves it, and you feel great and hilarious, you have done yourself and your character an injustice by not being true to the exercise. When we do push-ups, we shouldn't let our body sag or our shoulders crunch. That causes us to lose the integrity of the exercise, and we won't get stronger, we won't get better. We haven't worked the muscles this exercise is designed to develop. We love to be funny. It feels good. Don't worry. You will be funny, and what's even more, if you practice this properly, you will become engaging, which is much more long-lasting. So just let go of the funny for a minute. When we stop trying to control it and instead focus on being engaging and honest, organic funny moments have a tendency to pop up in a much more satisfying way.

You've learned how to work on this concept on your own, but if you are able to, this exercise is one where it is especially useful to have one or some partners to work with. It is often difficult to notice our actor habits, seeing as they are unconscious in the first place. Watch each other, and find these opportunities. Each time they notice you doing something other than walking and sitting in a chair, have them ask you why you are doing that. If you are on your own, take care to acknowledge these movements. Your fists are clenched - what are you holding? Is it a gift? A Flower? A dog leash? You keep adjusting your pants - are they falling down? Did a mouse run up your britches? You keep ducking to look where you are going (which is unnecessary, unless you are going under something) - is someone shooting at you?? Are you running a gambit? Notice that instead of just pointing out mistakes, you are making a game of it. Is that a present for me you're holding? Are you carrying something on your back that is making you hunch? Or, simpler, what is that? Are you okay? Are you cold? We do a lot of weird things without realizing it. It is great to have that outside eye to help us pinpoint them. Remember to celebrate our mistakes. They are what make us interesting.

The beauty of commedia and physical theatre is that every human actor mistake that we make is a theatrical opportunity. Use it. The audience already knows you've made a mistake, so don't hide it. That's selfish. Be generous. Notice your actor mistake as your character, and acknowledge it. Play with it. And share it with the audience. This exercise is one where we practice being genuine.

Keep in mind this genuineness also applies to frustration, stumbling, and anger as well. Stay true to your character, and embrace those moments. This exercise is designed to make you fail. We are never more human and genuine than when we are failing.

This is where the funny comes in. Go for it. Fail. Get frustrated. Try again. Fail again and again and again. Share all of it with your audience, and they will be completely engaged. When you bring them on this journey with you, they're on your team. They are going to feel everything that you feel, but from the comfort of sitting down. There is nothing more satisfying than laughing at yourself, but that can be very hard to do. So put yourself in that hot seat, be human, and they'll relate – and love every minute of it.

CHAPTER SEVEN

Lazzi

If there is one thing that is iconic about commedia dell'arte, it is the art of the "lazzo", better known as the "lazzi" (which is the plural word for lazzo). This is someone trying to pick up their hat, but accidentally kicking it away repeatedly. This is the chicken fight in *Family Guy*. A lazzo is a bit, a game, an exploration gone wild, it is a tangent we watch a character get lost in. A lazzo can be 5 seconds or 5 minutes long, but it does not affect the plot in any way. What differentiates a lazzo from a scene is that you could completely remove a lazzo and the plot would not be affected in any way whatsoever. You could insert a lazzo at any point, because again, it would not affect the story.

A classic example would be the famous "Arlecchino and the fly" lazzo. Arlecchino is going about whatever business he is on, in any show, and a fly lands on him. He goes to swat it, and it moves. The audience is engaged watching Arlecchino chase this fly about with his head (which is how the actor is portraying there being a fly, accompanied by the buzzing, of course), abusing himself as he swats at this fly until he either catches it, eats it, or it flies away (the last usually being the case). Then he continues on as if nothing has happened. This particular lazzo was well known, and could be pulled out at any moment, maybe to perk up the audience, or maybe because the actor forgot what came next and wanted to buy themselves some time (What? We NEVER do that…).

Although a show plot can survive without lazzi, commedia cannot. The lazzi are the magic glue of the show. They are moments for a character to show their true selves and play with the audience. They are moments that suck both actor and audience into the same place at the same moment.

There is a great exercise for working on developing lazzi, unimaginatively referred to as "the imagination game". It is a very simple, but boundless exercise. It is practiced on your own, although watching a few people do it side-by-side can yield some very interesting results. Begin by choosing a repeatable task or routine. For example, washing windows, or getting ready in the morning. You do not have to face any particular direction in the space, and you do not interact with anyone else in the space (if you are working with others) or anyone observing. This is not a performance exercise.

So you are repeating your task. You can repeat it as many times as you need to let that movement begin to inform you, instead of the other way around. This movement will grow into something else, something new, and follow it wherever it takes you. Vacuuming suddenly becomes a sword fight. Then that sword fight can take you away from that original repeated motion into a full-on battle, moving all over the place. Then, a new motion may take over and turn into fishing. That fish may yank you into the water and you become a submarine and discover Atlantis. Nothing is wrong in this exercise.

If you get stuck, don't worry. It will happen. Simply repeat the motion you are on until you are informed again, until something comes to you. If you don't know what your motion represents, that's fine. So you're pounding the floor and squeaking and you have no idea how the hell you got there? Great. Keep doing it. Something will come to you. It may take 10 minutes. It doesn't matter. You are training your brain to listen to your body. It is better to wait it out than to force it. When you force an action intellectually, that struggle will only close you off from your body.

Keep in mind that a scene may easily take you to another, such as the fish pulling you into the ocean, but also look for those repeatable motions. At the start, for example, if you chose baking cookies as your repeatable routine, instead of going from baking cookies to eating cookies to whatever, find one of the actions, such as stirring the batter or cracking the eggs, whatever sticks out to you, and have that become the repeating motion that propels you forward. Do this periodically throughout the exercise, in each scene you discover. If you don't know which motion to choose, repeat the scene until you find one that strikes your fancy and you want to explore. Now, this exercise at this point is endless. That can become a waking nightmare, so I will tell you how to cap it off.

After doing this exercise for years, I've grown to appreciate the value in how you finish this exercise. There are a lot of skills to be gained from it. Finishing is simple. Your aim is going to be to return to your original repeatable motion or routine, and then end in stillness.

This exercise can be any length. You may only get from vacuuming to a sword fight right back to vacuuming. You may take a full-blown journey. Any length is useful to practice. Don't get hung up on expectations. Don't hold yourself back. Especially if you are working with others in the space, don't feel pressured to stretch it out longer, or to finish more quickly. If you've finished before someone else, just stand in stillness and allow them to continue on. If you are last to finish, don't feel pressure. Allow yourself to find your way back organically.

Although this ending is contrary to the body-informing-the-brain, it is crucial to practice. This is what will save you when you are stuck on a tangent on stage, or when you must abandon a lazzo that just isn't working. Practice smoothing the rhythm and arc of your journey, building from the beginning, tapering back down to the end. You can try reversing back through the movements that got you to the peak, so you don't get caught up in manufacturing these movements too much. As you get more comfortable with this exercise, you'll find you know where you want to go, and you'll just allow your actions to get you there. And when in doubt, wait it out.

CHAPTER EIGHT

Building a Scene

You've learned about being on stage in commedia, wearing a mask, finding your voice, lazzi, saying yes, and having two masks on stage. Now it is time to begin building scenes.

You can begin with one or two-person scenes. Each come with their own difficulties, and benefits.

<u>For One Character:</u>

The most basic exercise you can do is to find a reason to exit. Block out a space to act as your stage, and make sure it is clear when you are on, and where it is clear you have exited. Outside the space, put on your mask, find the body, find the voice, and enter. Enter with purpose. Later on you can play with accidental entrances or being surprised to find yourself in front of an audience, but for the purpose of this exercise, imagine your character knows exactly where they are going, what they are doing, and why they are here. Maybe you are teaching a fencing lesson, or are just arriving in the theatre to watch a movie. Make this clear with your body and actions. Try to not simply verbally give it to your audience ("ah, here I am in this movie theatre"). Simply be in that space as that character. Interact with your audience. Remember, share everything with them. Be generous. They are there with you.

Then comes the tricky part: your exit. In commedia, never, ever leave the stage without a reason. A good, strong, clear reason. Everything in commedia on stage is a choice with a drive, and until you are off that stage, you are still making choices, including why you are leaving that space. Being done with a conversation is not a reason to exit. I am being shot at, my kitchen is on fire, I'm covered in fire ants, I've just been killed. These are all reasons to exit. Arlecchino may chase a pie that has been thrown off stage. Pantalone would chase a coin. Capitano, who was teaching a sword lesson, accidentally tossed his foil into the air, and he must run off stage, terrified of the sharp pointed object falling down towards him. The audience knows that the character has exited. It was noticed as strongly as the tulip on the blank page. They also know what to or what from they are going. The drive is clear. Do not exit until you have a reason to exit. Exiting is an action, meaning you will have the focus. If you are going to make everyone stop and watch you, then you had better make it interesting. Be the prettiest damn tulip on that stage.

<u>Two to Tango:</u>

Make sure before you jump right into scene-building that you have been practicing the chair exercise plentifully, especially if you are planning to bring two masks on stage. Focus is crucially important here. Remember you are saying yes to your partner here as well, and then you need to support them as well when you can. Think of this as the imagination exercise, but not only are you movements informing you, but your partner also may yank you in a new direction. Don't resist it, and don't try to force it into your idea either. Take the opportunities to see where you both end up.

The two person exercise is just like the one person exercise, only you have less control (which you shouldn't grasp for in commedia anyway), and you have a lot more technically to pay attention to. You do, however, on the bright side, now have a buddy up there with you, a lifeline, someone to save you, or at least suffer alongside you.

You are going to find a reason to exit. Before you can do that, however, you must enter the space to begin with. Once you are both prepared, remember the focus game, and enter the space. Now, your characters aren't just walking about and happen upon this space with your audience. Why are you there? This can be decided beforehand at first, at least a general scenario, but I challenge you to enter blindly. One person begins an action (with purpose) and it is either clear, which their partner may then build on, or it is not, which allows the partner to dictate what it is. Sure, the partner could ask them what they are doing, but where's the fun in that? The first person may think they've begun building a tent, but when the partner joins in and exclaims, "Gee, this is a really weird way to make cookies," it is clear that you are headed in a new direction. Go with it. Have fun throwing each other off-kilter, but make sure that it is not at your partner's expense. Give them material to work on and jump off of. When you freak out and don't know what to do, pass the focus. When your partner is freaking out and passes you the focus, help them out. When you are both freaking out, pass that focus back and forth like a mad ping-pong game until one of you thinks of something or something happens. Remember you have an audience there. Remember your technique. Remember your drives. Be in the space, be present, be there for your partner, and explore. Then find a reason to exit.

One of the most important things to pay attention to when you have two masks on stage is, what is their relationship? Servant-master? Master-master? Two lovers? The more clearly the relationship is defined, the clearer it is how your character would behave and react, which helps you on stage and helps you understand your character more. Their hierarchies are what commedia dell'arte is about. It is about people. It comments on social status and society. It is less about the plot, and more about the characters. The reason it is so important to make clear, strong choices is not to clarify the story, but to clarify who these characters are. The reason the actions must be clear is to show what is driving them. That is what we relate to. We may not all eat a chicken whole, like Zanni, but we know what it is to be hungry.

CHAPTER NINE

Social Relevancy

A lot of times, when you tell someone that you are performing "commedia dell'arte", one of a few things is likely to happen. Either they have seen something of it before, maybe covered it as part of a drama class, and you will immediately be categorized into that obscure little corner of theatre, with weird masks and old, 17th century-style, billowy costumes and posturing. Or, they may not have heard of it, and they Google "commedia dell'arte" and up pops the beautiful, but extremely traditional, historical pictures of commedia characters. Or, they've seen commedia before, good or bad, but most likely a bit different from what you are intending to do, simply because everyone has their own style. Hopefully not, but you might come up against people thinking of studying or performing commedia as an exploration of something traditional and old. Dated.

If we are true to the original form and the purpose it served, that should not be the case at all. Commedia emerged as the people's theatre, performed on the streets and covering topics that were otherwise untouchable. They were political. They were social. They covered issues that everyone of that time could relate to and what was going on in the community. So, if you were able to find an account of a performance that went on then, and were to perform it today, it likely wouldn't be specifically relevant, though it might hold some core topics, and a lot of the references wouldn't make sense. You would be performing essentially a nice historical reenactment of a traditional commedia dell'arte performance from the 17th, 18th, or whichever century it took place. That can be particularly fascinating as well, but that's not the commedia that is being explored here.

Commedia does not have to be dated. It *shouldn't* be dated. Commedia is about people today, and the things that we all struggle with. This can be portrayed with modern versions of some of the previously created characters (Arlecchino, Pantalone, Pulcinella), or with new ones following the same form, or even a combination of the two. The truth is, the character, and archetypes previously used, are still very relevant today. That is what is so beautifully adaptable about it. However, we do have new archetypes that have emerged in our modern societies. But that is covered more where we discuss characters and the masks. We also must think about context and your canovaccio (don't worry, we'll go over "canovaccio", but for now just think "script"). Or even your sketches and lazzi.

At the base of commedia dell'arte is a grouping

of human issues. These included things like hunger, sexual appetite, money (in the form of currency or just personal gain), and pride. These are needs that practically any human can relate to, and these drives are relevant across class, age, race, gender, and even time. These always have been and probably always will be relevant issues and driving forces motivating all of our choices and actions. Not that every person is driven by all of them, but there is usually at least one predominant drive bringing someone through life. This is essential to commedia characters. Anytime you are working on your feet and developing a character or scene, find which one of these drives is moving you from point A to point B. At no point should you be doing something on stage simply because it has to happen to drive the plot. Everything is a choice, as we've discussed, and these choices are motivated by these drives, unless something stronger overpowers it. For example, Arlecchino ducking to avoid being hit by Pantalone is not driven by hunger, but self-preservation is a pretty strong, instinctual drive, and is therefore an acceptable exception to the drives rule. Keep in mind, this deviation is a result of a stronger drive pulling the character from their primary one, not simply them drifting of away from that original drive. Anything else is just not enough. Curiosity is not a strong enough choice. Arlecchino is curious by nature, sure, but he would only deviate from his path because either, for example, A) he has been startled by something, and that causes him to explore it (self-preservation leading to distraction), or B) he thinks there may be food or whatever his drive is at the end of that journey of curiosity.

Exiting simply because the scene is over is unacceptable. If you are leaving, that is a choice. You are being shot at, your house is on fire, your love is just on the other side of that wall and is calling you – these are all reasons to leave.

Thinking in terms of drives makes it clear that commedia dell'arte is still relevant in today's world. You just have to think in more modern terms. Arlecchino isn't chasing after a roast chicken, crust of bread and mead – it's probably McDonald's, a doughnut, and maybe a beer. Pantalone isn't a wealthy merchant in Venice bringing in spices from the Far East, he's Mr. Burns, a powerful CEO running a nuclear facility. Pulcinella isn't working the fields, he's working the computer in a field of cubicles.

Then we get to bigger messages and arcs that may be touched on. You should have a good idea of what's going on in the world, and if not, get Twitter. Use the internet. Commedia today isn't making fun of the local corrupt bishop, it points at the local congressman, or Chick-Fil-A. Today, commedia can start discussions about the homeless, which are just as relevant now as they ever were. It can talk about women being jailed for miscarriages, corporations sucking the life out of their employees, about mortgages, and about the mechanic that rips you off. This is what commedia grew up doing, and in order for it to be relevant today, and not die again, it needs to continue this, and adapt. Commedia shouldn't exist only as a performance art as it did like a preserved museum exhibit. There is already enough of that in books and in the actual museum exhibits. As a modern form of performance, it is a powerful tool that we can wield, and it would be a shame to see it go to waste.

CHAPTER TEN

Canovaccio

You've now gone through the basics, how to wear a mask, find its body and voice. You've been practicing lazzi, and how to build scenes. If you want to have a full performance, then the next thing you need to know about is a "canovaccio".

As commedia dell'arte is all about improvisation, reaction, and interaction, it does not have a written script. There are no written instructions on what to say and do once you are on stage. What we have instead is a canovaccio.

A canovaccio is essentially a listing of plot points and scenes. It is the dots in a connect-the-dots picture. Creating the lines that build the full picture is up to you. It would look something like this:

Little Red Riding Hood

- Little Red/Mother
    o Mother sends Red to deliver basket to grandmother
    o Gives directions
- Little Red
    o Exploring forest
- Little Red/Wolf

- Little Red/"Grandmother" Wolf
  o "What big eyes you have!"
- Hunter enters
  o Wolf killed

As you can see, there is not much detail, and no lines written, unless there is something that must be consistently said (i.e. "What big eyes you have!"). Each point lists the characters in the scene, and basically what happens.

This would be the starting point for rehearsals. You know who enters, and you know the basic plot point that needs to happen. Now you get to play. Now comes scene building and finding a reason to exit. The more you get to know your character, the more you know how they would react in each situation. As this happens, you show begins to flesh out.

Your canovaccio may change as you are playing and devising, and you should let it. A hard lesson we have learned in Tut'Zanni is to not only say yes to everything, but to be able to let something go if it is not serving the show, especially in development. You will find moments, jokes, and choices that you love, and you can't bear to see them go, but you must. This will actually provide more freedom to explore other directions. Also, frequently, the good stuff finds its way back in, so trust the process. If they find their way back in, then more often than not they fit better, and since you've explored everything else, you can be sure of your choice. This way, everyone trusts it now.

Commedia is most successful as an unselfish form. You must support each other, and think of the show as a whole. If you don't help each other, any failures on stage will affect everyone. If energy drops and urgency is lost, then is it everyone's responsibility to get it back. Failures and successes are equally shared. If someone went a direction you didn't want to go, let it go, say yes, and see where you end up. It's not about any one individual character; commedia is about relationships between all the characters.

As your canovaccio develops, plot point will come and go, but it will never take the shape of a script. You may add in details like "slap lazzo" or "get pen from audience" because these are important points to remember, but it will remain a list of points. It can be scary to not have something as sure as a script, but each night you have a new audience and a new energy. You need to play with those. A joke is never funny the third time. Moments repeated too many times become stale. Let each performance be fresh and new. Sure, you will inevitably repeat some things from one night to the next. If something works well, you *should* use it. But don't just leave it there, pay attention to it. See how it is feeling each night, and when it starts to fade, move away from it. Let it go. Find something new. A commedia show is like a living thing, constantly growing, changing, adapting. This is exciting. It makes it personal, an inside joke unique to each specific audience, a journey you only take with them.

Be open and adaptable, and it will be one of the most satisfying and rewarding adventures you can take, both for yourself and your audience.

AN OVERVIEW

Basics and Fundamentals

There are some basic concepts that you will want to keep in mind at all times. These concepts have been explored in depth in the other chapters, but let this be your checklist when you are working:

<u>Be aware.</u> Be present. Pay attention. This seems obvious, but there is so much to pay attention to at all times. It is what will mentally exhaust you the most in front of an audience, or kill you if you don't, so make sure to work out this muscle.

<u>Be engaged.</u> Know where your body is and what it is doing at all times. You should know what every bit of you is up to, from your eyes to your fingertips. Remember that every movement is a choice, and commedia characters are always economical. This means you should have a neutral, engaged stance when you are not currently making a choice, such as when you are giving a partner on stage focus, or are just about to make a move.

<u>Where is the focus?</u> If the audience's eyes were lasers, they should always all be converging on the same point, and as that point moves, you are responsible for where it goes (it is your job to guide it). And, just as much as you certainly don't want your audience to be closing their eyes, that point should always be somewhere.

<u>Be relevant.</u> Commedia dell'arte isn't just a piece of art being presented at an audience. It is a communication. So discuss things that are interesting and relatable, in terms that the audience will understand. Commedia isn't' preachy; it's truthful, honest, and unpolished. It is a way to laugh at our miseries so that maybe we'll pay attention to or talk about them. Make commedia matter, and it will stick around, and so will you as an artist.

<u>Be generous.</u> Your audience came to be a part of this conversation. Give it to them. Bring them in. Share all your moments with them, and listen to them. This makes you a team, and who isn't going to root for themselves? If you make them a part of this journey, they will only want you to succeed.

Say yes. Fail. I would say this is part of being generous, but it is so important, it needs to be its own checkpoint. The only thing that is going to hold you back from your best work is yourself. Be willing to fail. Know that you *will* fail. And do it. Go for it. Say yes. Commedia and its characters are beautifully human, complete with fallacies, awkwardness, and being bad at stuff. Own it. Acknowledge it. If you are keeping all the above fundamentals, you will find the joy of failing. Flop.

A Note About Tut'Zanni

In 2011, I finally decided to follow one of my dreams and start a theatre company of my own. I travelled to Italy where I asked Dory to be my co-founder. I was thrilled that she jumped on board, and we roped along Patrick, Allegra, Liam, and finally Molly. For over 5 years now, I have had the joy and the honor of working, teaching, and creating with them across the world. We are exploring what Commedia dell'Arte can be today, and what we can do with it. I am constantly learning, and I hope that you can gain something from what I have to share.

About the Author

ALi Landvatter is the founder of the acclaimed U.S.-based commedia dell'arte troupe, Tut'Zanni Theatre Company. She attended the Accademia dell'Arte, where she met her company members and worked with such instructors as Marcello Bartoli and Kevin Crawford. ALi frequently acts as a guest artist and clinician at universities and schools across the country in addition to a regular performance schedule including both national and international appearances.

CPSIA information can be obtained
at www.ICGtesting.com
Printed in the USA
LVHW091518091221
705747LV00003B/629